Review

Use these words to fill in the blank spaces in the sentences. You will need to use some more than once:

after, at, away, back, down, for, from, in, into, of, off, on, out, over, through, to, up, with.

1. When her father went ________________ to buy something, she looked ________________ the store for him.
2. She has been living ________________ Taiwan ________________ several years.
3. "Take ________________ those wet clothes," said her mother, "and put ________________ some dry ones."
4. "There's something wrong ________________ this pen. I can't write ________________ it."
5. Please bring ________________ the book to me when you have finished ________________ it.
6. When clothes are worn ________________ they have to be thrown ________________ .
7. I borrowed this pen ________________ my sister and I picked ________________ the pencil in the playground.
8. The man walked ________________ the steps to the street below and got ________________ a car. Then he drove ________________ .
9. You must be careful when you get ________________ a bus. You may be run ________________ by a car.
10. We leave home ________________ eight o'clock ________________ the morning.
11. The airplane was flying ________________ London to New York. It landed ________________ Kennedy Airport.
12. Vacation begins ________________ Friday. We will not come to school ________________ six weeks.
13. Do not cross ________________ a mistake. Put a line ________________ it.
14. He is ten years ________________ age and very good ________________ baseball.
15. He was knocked ________________ by a bus and, while he was lying in the street, he was run ________________ by a car. They took him ________________ the hospital ________________ an ambulance.

Review

Finish each sentence by adding the correct form of the word underlined in the other sentence.

1. He was a foolish boy. He behaved ________________ in class.
2. His words were very clear. He spoke very ________________ .
3. He ate his food hungrily. He was a ________________ boy.
4. She spoke in a soft voice. She spoke ________________ .
5. He knows how to spell. His ________________ is very good.
6. They were noisy children. They went into the classroom very ________________ .
7. Her work was always neat. She always did it ________________ .
8. Luckily the car did not hit him. He was very ________________ .
9. She was very interested in the book. She thought it was very ________________ .
10. The orange was full of juice. It was very ________________ .
11. She was gentle with small children. She treated them ________________ .
12. It was a fierce lion. It roared ________________ .
13. He did not take care with his work. He did it ________________ .
14. We all enjoyed the picnic. It was very ________________ .
15. It was an easy addition problem and I did it ________________ .
16. The room was very ________________ . There was dust everywhere.
17. He was a dangerous driver. He drove ________________ .
18. She did everything cheerfully. She was always ________________ .
19. It was a very ________________ journey. We were all very tired by the end.
20. The movie made them very excited. It was a very ________________ movie.
21. We are going to meet at five o'clock. The ________________ is at five o'clock.
22. His leg gave him a lot of pain. It was very ________________ .

Review

Write true answers to the questions using **often** *or* **never**.

1. Have you ever been on a train?

Yes, I have often been on a train.

2. Have you ever seen a dog with two heads?

No, I have never seen a dog with two heads.

3. Have you ever seen a train?

____

4. Have you ever been in an airplane?

____

5. Have you ever been in the ocean?

____

6. Have you ever fallen into a river?

____

7. Have you ever eaten an egg?

____

8. Have you ever held a snake?

____

9. Have you ever helped your mother?

____

10. Have you ever been to the movies?

____

11. Have you ever seen the moon?

____

12. Have you ever been to England?

____

Review

Write answers to the questions beginning with **No** *and using* **yet** *and* **almost**.

1. Have you finished writing yet?

No, I have not finished writing yet but I have almost finished.

2. Has she finished singing yet?

No, she has not finished singing yet but she has almost finished.

3. Have you finished reading yet?

No, ______________________________ .

4. Has she finished sewing yet?

____

5. Has he finished drawing yet?

____

6. Have they finished playing baseball yet?

____

7. Have they finished cleaning the room yet?

____

8. Have you finished polishing your shoes yet?

____

9. Has the man finished fixing the faucet yet?

____

10. Have the girls finished painting yet?

____

11. Have you finished this page yet?

____

12. Has Mrs. Mitchell finished cooking yet?

____

Review

Choose the word or words, given in parentheses, that best complete the sentence and write your answer in the blank space.

1. At the corner of the street there was a police officer ________________ duty. (in, at, with, for, on)

2. You can buy that dog if you want to. It is ________________ sale. (to, in, with, for, at)

3. They would not let me ________________ with them. They made me ________________ home. (went, to go, going, go, gone) (went, to go, going, go, gone)

4. He wanted ________________ the answer but she would not ________________ him. (know, knowing, to know, knew) (told, tell, telling, to tell)

5. We could hear someone ________________ the piano when we arrived. (to play, played, playing, play)

6. The laborers took ________________ their coats and began to dig ________________ the road. (off, out, on, away, from) (out, up, on, to, over)

7. I enjoy ________________ but I hate ________________ underwater. (swim, swimming, to swim, swam) (go, going, went)

8. He likes to sit at the back of the class, ________________ ? (doesn't he, isn't he, don't he, isn't it, is it)

9. It's going to rain, ________________ it? (doesn't, isn't, won't, does, will)

10. She didn't give you your money back, ________________ ? (did she, isn't it, is she, isn't she, won't she)

11. You won't tell anyone, ________________ ? (won't you, will you, isn't it, is it, do you)

12. You've finished the page now, ________________ ? (isn't it, haven't you, did you, didn't you, won't you)

Review

In each space write the correct form of the word given in parentheses.

1. It is a lovely day and the sun ________________ . (shine)
2. She ________________ an English lesson every day. (have)
3. My brother and I ________________ to a new school yesterday. (go)
4. I often ________________ with a pen and I ________________ with one now. (write)
5. We ________________ to take a vacation next month. (go)
6. Last week I ________________ a bad cold. (have)
7. Yesterday I ________________ at the back of the class. (sit)
8. Last night we ________________ our teacher in the supermarket. (see)
9. When we get home from school we usually ________________ a meal before we do our homework. (have)
10. Our vacation ________________ last Friday. (begin)
11. "You can't have the apple." "It's too late. I ________________ it." (eat)
12. When I passed her window, she ________________ . (sing)
13. He asked me whether I ________________ the man. (know)
14. The teacher will not let him go until he ________________ the exercise again. (write)
15. I will stay here until you ________________ . (finish)
16. There is a hole in his shirt where he ________________ it. (tear)
17. She never ________________ where she is going. One day she ________________ an accident. (look, have)

Review

Choose the word or words, given in parentheses, that best complete the sentence and write your answer in the blank space.

1. He eats a lot of candy because he ________________ it.
(likes, is liking, like, liked, liking)

2. When she wakes up, she ________________ out of bed.
(is getting, got, gets, get, has got)

3. If it ________________, we will not go.
(will rain, was raining, rain, rains, rained)

4. Is this the book ________________ you were looking for?
(that, who, what, where, it)

5. I want to find the man ________________ sold me this fish.
(which, who, what, he, him)

6. Two hours ago it ________________ but now it has stopped.
(rains, raining, rained, was raining, has rained)

7. When the car turned over, Mr. Wilson ________________ it.
(was driving, drove, has driven, is driving, drives)

8. There is ________________ sand on the beach.
(a lot of, a great many, several, many, a few)

9. There are ________________ cars in New York.
(much, a great deal of, a large amount of, many, very much)

10. ________________ we go home now or do you want to stay a little longer?
(Are, Should, Let's, Have, Will)

11. ________________ do you come to school, by bus or car?
(Which, How, Where, May, What)

12. I ________________ be able to go tomorrow but I am not sure.
(can, will, am, may, must)

1. 2. 3. 4. 5.

6. 7. 8. 9. 10.

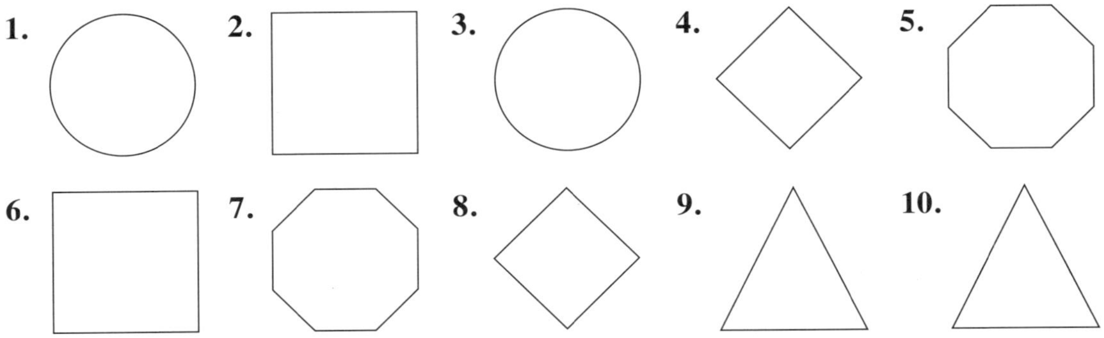

Write four sentences using **the same as** *and four using* **different from**.

1. No. 1 is the same as No. 3.
2. No. 2 is different from No. 1.
3. ___
4. ___
5. ___
6. ___
7. ___
8. ___
9. ___
10. ___

Make sentences using **like** *and the words given.*

1. stream — river (smaller)
2. ship — boat (bigger)
3. road — highway (shorter)
4. bush — tree (smaller)
5. hut — house (smaller)
6. town — village (bigger)

1. A stream is like a river but it's smaller.
2. ___
3. ___
4. ___
5. ___
6. ___

Finish the sentences using **like**.

1. 

(swam) She swam like a fish.

2. 

(cried) The little boy cried ______________________________ .

3. 

(sang) Marie ______________________________ .

4. 

(sank) The ship ______________________________ .

5. 

(climbed) The boys ______________________________ .

Can you find the words? Write the first letter of each word in the boxes.

 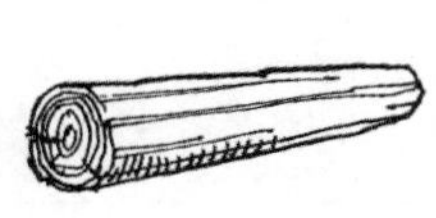   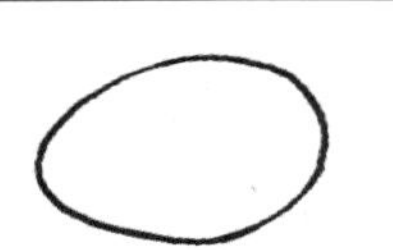

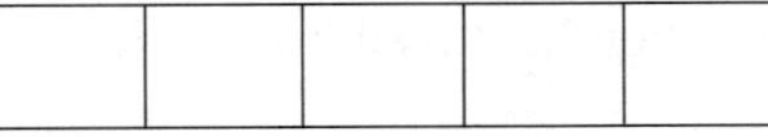

    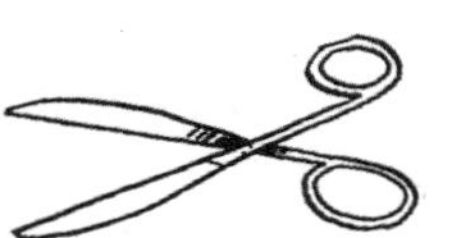

UNIT 2

Change the sentences using **since** *with the words given in parentheses.*

1. He moved to this country in July. (has lived)
   He has lived in this country since July.
2. I heard that song last when I was seven. (have not heard)
   I have not heard that song since I was seven.
3. He bought the car in September. (has had)
   ____
4. She saw him last year. (has not seen)
   ____
5. She visited her mother last in 1985. (has not visited)
   ____
6. He left home at seven o'clock. (has not been)
   ____
7. He borrowed the book last Thursday. (has had)
   ____
8. She became sick last December. (has been)
   ____
9. She first used that pencil in January. (has used)
   ____
10. She began carrying that bag at four o'clock. (has carried)
    ____
11. He began collecting stamps when he was a boy. (has collected)
    ____
12. He played baseball last in 1992. (has not played)
    ____

I They You We	have been here	for	half an hour. one hour. ten minutes. three days.
		since	eleven o'clock. breakfast time. yesterday. the end of last month.

Write four sentences using **for** *and four sentences using* **since**.

1. ______________________________

2. ______________________________

3. ______________________________

4. ______________________________

1. ______________________________

2. ______________________________

3. ______________________________

4. ______________________________

Add **for** *or* **since** *to these sentences.*

1. We have been waiting ________________ two hours.

2. I have not seen a newspaper ________________ last week.

3. She has worked in that office ________________ two years.

4. I have not seen him ________________ a long time.

5. She has been our teacher ________________ the beginning of the term.

6. They have been here ________________ an hour and a half.

7. He has not been home ________________ last Friday.

8. I will not see my home again ________________ three years.

UNIT 3

Make sentences using **have to**, **will have to**, *and* **had to**.

1. do this exercise now

   I have to do this exercise now.

2. stay at home tomorrow

   I will have to stay at home tomorrow.

3. do some homework last night

   I had to do some homework last night.

4. wait for my mother now

   ____

5. help my father tomorrow

   ____

6. stay in bed yesterday

   ____

7. go to school now

   ____

8. go to see a doctor tomorrow

   ____

9. go to the city yesterday

   ____

10. go home now

    ____

11. leave school one day

    ____

12. do a lot of work yesterday

    ____

In the passages below there is no punctuation or capitalization. Write each passage out in the space given, putting in all the punctuation marks and capital letters.

1. look at me said miss lane what am I holding in my hand
david put his hand up I think its a flower he said
very good said the teacher what kind of flower is it
it isnt a real flower said jean its made of paper

____

____

____

____

____

____

____

2. a number of people were standing by the side of the road
what has happened a police officer asked them
I cant see one of the people said I think there has been an accident
move away please the police officer said let me have a look

____

____

____

____

____

____

____

Write sentences about the pictures. Use these words:

not enough **too much** **too many**

1. **coffee – pot**
   There is not enough coffee in the pot.

2. **water – bucket**
   There is too much ____ .

3. **apples – plate**
   There are ____ .

4. **wheels – car**
   There are not ____ .

5. **people – car**
   ____

6. **water – boat**
   ____

7. **water – glass**
   ____

8. **ink – bottle**
   ____

9. books – desk

____

10. rice – plate

____

11. pens – pocket

____

12. rings – hand

____

13. people – ship

____

14. tea – cup

____

Finish these sentences by adding **enough, not enough, too many,** *or* **too much**.

1. One orange is ______________ for ten people.
2. Ten oranges are ______________ for one boy.
3. One ruler is ______________ to draw a line.
4. A bag of rice is ______________ for one meal.
5. A hundred students are ______________ for one classroom.
6. One chair is ______________ for one person.

UNIT 5

Combine the sentences using **too**.

1. She cannot work. She is too tired.

   She is too tired to work.

2. He cannot go through the door. He is too fat.

   ____

3. The stick will not break. It is too thick.

   ____

4. He could not work. He was too lazy.

   ____

5. He could not see over the wall. He was too small.

   ____

6. She did not make a mistake. She was too clever.

   ____

7. The box will not go under the table. It is too big.

   ____

8. The piece of paper will not go into the desk. It is too wide.

   ____

9. The ruler will not go into my bag. It is too long.

   ____

10. No one can carry the bag. It is too heavy.

    ____

11. No one could answer the question. It was too hard.

    ____

12. They could not speak. They were too frightened.

    ____

Combine the sentences using **too . . . for . . . to . . . .**

1. The box was too big. Jim could not carry it.

   The box was too big for Jim to carry.

2. The chair was too big. Eva could not lift it.

   ____

3. The writing was too small. We could not read it.

   ____

4. The shirt is too small. I cannot wear it.

   ____

5. The problem was too difficult. The children could not do it.

   ____

6. The book is too difficult. He cannot read it.

   ____

7. The stick is too thick. She cannot break it.

   ____

8. The box was too wide. We could not carry it through the door.

   ____

9. The dot was too small. We could not see it.

   ____

10. The bag was too heavy. They could not carry it.

    ____

11. Her writing is too bad. The teacher cannot read it.

    ____

12. There were too many books. We could not count them.

    ____

UNIT 6

Combine the sentences using **enough**.

1. Make twelve good sentences.

   The boy was tall enough to see over the wall.

2. The girl was small. She could get through the window.

   ____

3. The horse was fast. It could win the race.

   ____

4. He was not big. He could not carry the box.

   ____

5. The rope was strong. It could hold four men.

   ____

6. The room was not big. It could not hold fifty people.

   ____

7. The boat was big. It could hold twenty people.

   ____

8. The boat was not big. It could not go far out to sea.

   ____

9. The clothes were not heavy. They did not keep the children warm.

   ____

10. Mike was not tall. He could not reach the window.

    ____

11. Eva's sister was not old enough. She could not go to school.

    ____

12. The package was small. It went into the mailbox.

    ____

Write the missing sentences. Be careful with punctuation marks.

1. It is Bob's book. It belongs to Bob.
2. It is Sarah's pen. It belongs ______________ .
3. It is Mr. Vega's money. ______________________________
4. They are my brother's books. ______________________________
5. They are the farmer's cows. ______________________________
6. The pencil belongs to Alan. It is Alan's pencil.
7. The shoe belongs to Terry. ______________________________
8. The money belongs to the little girl. ______________________________
9. The flowers belong to my brother. They ______________________________ .
10. The pen belongs to the teacher. ______________________________

Write the words spoken. Be careful with punctuation marks.

1. I am working. "I'm working," said Joe.
2. She is running. "______________________________," he said.
3. You are tall. "______________________________," said Mrs. Gray.
4. They are reading. ______________________________ she said.
5. It is raining. ______________________________ he said.
6. We are coming! ______________________________ they shouted.

UNIT 7

I do not know Can you tell me Ask your teacher You must find out	what	to do. to write. to read. to say.

Write different sentences using this table. Use a question mark when necessary.

1. ______________________________
2. ______________________________
3. ______________________________
4. ______________________________
5. ______________________________
6. ______________________________
7. ______________________________
8. ______________________________
9. ______________________________
10. ______________________________
11. ______________________________
12. ______________________________

Please tell me Do you know No one knows The teacher told us	where when how	to do it. to start. to begin. to carry it.

Write five sentences using **where**, *five sentences using* **when**, *and five sentences using* **how**. *Use a question mark when necessary.*

1. ______________________________

2. ______________________________

3. ______________________________

4. ______________________________

5. ______________________________

6. ______________________________

7. ______________________________

8. ______________________________

9. ______________________________

10. ______________________________

11. ______________________________

12. ______________________________

13. ______________________________

14. ______________________________

15. ______________________________

UNIT 8

Underline the best answer.

1. Alan says that he is / was twelve years old.

2. The teacher said that the answers are / were right.

3. I think that oranges are / were better than apples.

4. Jack said that he wants / wanted to go home.

5. Bob said that he knows / knew what to do.

6. They know that there is / was going to be a holiday.

7. I think it is / was going to rain today.

8. Everyone thought that the pictures are / were beautiful.

9. No one knows that the window is / was broken.

10. Everyone knew that answer is / was wrong.

11. She said that she wants / wanted an ice cream cone.

12. She says that she wants / wanted an ice cream cone.

Read No. 1 and No. 2. Then change the other sentences in the same way.

1. "It is hot," said Jim.

Jim said that it was hot.

2. "I want something to drink," said Marie

Marie said that she wanted something to drink.

3. "It is very nice," said Mrs. Vega.

____

4. "The water is warm," said Kathy.

____

5. "I want to go home," said Mr. Wilson.

____

6. "I like candy," said Mike.

____

7. "It's ten o'clock," said Mr. Mitchell.

____

8. "I want more orange juice," said Jean.

____

9. "It is going to rain," said Mr. Vega.

____

10. "We like swimming," said the boys.

____

11. "We don't like walking," said the girls.

____

12. "I feel cold," said Mrs. Johnson.

____

UNIT 9

Complete the sentences. The first four are done for you.

1. What is it? I don't know what it is.
2. What are they doing? I will ask them what they are doing.
3. What has he done? Don't you know what he has done?
4. What does he want? I don't know what he wants.
5. What is it? I will find out ______________________________.
6. What is her name? I will ask her ______________________________.
7. What are they doing? I don't know ______________________________.
8. What is he saying? I don't know ______________________________.
9. What are they reading? I can't see ______________________________.
10. What has he done? No one knows ______________________________.
11. What have they written? I will ask them ______________________________.
12. What will he do? No one knows ______________________________.
13. What will they find? No one knows ______________________________.
14. What can we do? I don't know ______________________________.
15. What can they see? Ask them ______________________________.
16. What does he want? I will ask him ______________________________.
17. What do they want? I don't know ______________________________.
18. What did he find? I don't know ______________________________.
19. What did he make? He won't tell me ______________________________.
20. What did they sing? I will ask them ______________________________.
21. What did he do? I don't know ______________________________.
22. What is she doing? I can't see ______________________________.
23. What is she saying? I can't hear ______________________________.
24. What will you do? I don't know ______________________________.

Review

Add periods, question marks, quotation marks, and commas where they are needed.

1. “That is Terry’s desk, said the teacher.
2. “What are you looking for ” asked his mother.
3. The money is on the table, said his mother
4. Jack asked, Where are you going
5. We re going home now they said
6. Mrs. Arnold said to Jack Where did you put the eraser
7. That s my pen said Marie I ve lost mine said Kathy.
8. You re late said the teacher Where have you been
9. It s four o clock said Mr. Gray It s time to go home
10. What s the man s name he asked

Choose the best answer.

1.	When I was small, I	like liked was liking	to look at picture books.
2.	We can go home when this lesson	will finish. is finishing. is finished.	
3.	It was cold yesterday,	is it? isn’t it? wasn’t it?	
4.	When it	is is being will be	hot, I like to swim in the ocean.
5.	A hundred books are	too much too many enough	for one person to carry.
6.	We have not finished the exercise	already. yet. soon.	

Complete the sentences.

1. He did not know how she did it.
   He asked her how she did it.
2. We wanted to find out how he made it.
   We asked him ______________________________.
3. The teacher wanted to know how he fell down.
   She asked him ______________________________.
4. We did not know how she went there.
   We asked her ______________________________.
5. His mother did not know how he tore his shirt.
   He told her ______________________________.
6. The teacher asked him how he cut his finger.
   The teacher wanted ______________________________.
7. Her mother asked her how she knocked over the glass.
   Her mother wanted ______________________________.
8. The police officer wanted to know how the man stole the money.
   The police officer tried to find out ______________________________.
9. We did not understand how he could carry the big box.
   We asked ______________________________.
10. We did not know how she glued the pieces together.
    She told us ______________________________.
11. We did not know how he found it.
    He told ______________________________.
12. They did not know how it got there.
    They wanted ______________________________.

Read No. 1 and No. 2. Then change the other sentences in the same way.

1. "How high is the tree?" Jim asked Mr. Gray.
   Jim asked Mr. Gray how high the tree was.
2. "How tall is Terry?" Miss Lane asked Jean.
   Miss Lane asked Jean how tall Terry was.
3. "How old is David?" Marie asked Sarah.
   ____
4. "How long is the ruler?" Mrs. Arnold asked Joe.
   ____
5. "How big is the boat?" Bob asked his father.
   ____
6. "How wide is the river?" Eva asked her mother.
   ____

Read No. 1 and No. 2. Then change the other sentences in the same way.

1. "How did you make the kite?" Mike asked Alan.
   Mike asked Alan how he made the kite.
2. "How did you come to school?" Mrs. Arnold asked Jack.
   Mrs. Arnold asked Jack how he came to school.
3. "How did you make the cake?" Mary asked her mother.
   ____
4. "How did you lose your bag?" Mrs. Gray asked Marie.
   ____
5. "How did you find the store?" we asked Joe.
   ____
6. "How did you break your arm?" they asked Mr. Wilson.
   ____

Answer the questions beginning with the words given. The first two are done for you.

1. When is he going home?

   I don't know when he is going home.

2. When will they paint the door?

   I will ask them when they will paint the door.

3. When are they coming back?

   They cannot tell us ______________________________.

4. When can you come to see me?

   I will tell you tomorrow ______________________________.

5. When will he do it?

   He is not sure ______________________________.

6. When is she going to stop singing?

   We don't know ______________________________.

7. When does the sun rise?

   I will find out when ______________________________.

8. When does the mail carrier come to the school?

   I cannot tell you ______________________________.

9. When will vacation begin?

   Ask your teacher ______________________________.

10. When are you going to buy a new coat?

    You must ask my mother ______________________________.

11. What time does he get home?

    I will ask him what time ______________________________.

12. When will she tell us a story?

    I don't know ______________________________.

UNIT
12

Write sentences beginning with the words in parentheses.

1. Where are the children? (I don't know)
   I don't know where the children are.
2. Where is David? (I don't know)
   ____
3. Where is the bus going? (I'll ask someone)
   ____
4. Where are the books? (Do you know)
   ____
5. Where does she go to school? (I don't know)
   ____
6. Where does he keep his bicycle? (Ask him)
   ____
7. Where do the children play? (Please tell me)
   ____
8. Where did David go? (Does anyone know)
   ____
9. Where did they find the little boy? (I don't know)
   ____
10. Where did the car go? (Did you see)
    ____
11. Where can I find a doctor? (Does anyone know)
    ____
12. Where will they go tomorrow? (I don't know)
    ____

Can anyone tell me Do you know No one knows We will try to find out Someone told me Someone will tell me I don't know Please tell me I can't understand They want to know	why	he did it. they were late. she said that. the house caught on fire. she would not come. he did not come to school. she did not do her homework. the car hit the wall. the bus turned over. that taxi would not stop. we have to go home. he had to do the exercise again. no one came to the door. the package did not arrive. the school was closed. the pen won't write.

Write sentences using the table on page 30. Use question marks where necessary.

1. Someone told me why he did not come to school.
2. ______________________________
3. ______________________________
4. ______________________________
5. ______________________________
6. ______________________________
7. ______________________________
8. ______________________________
9. ______________________________
10. ______________________________
11. ______________________________
12. ______________________________
13. ______________________________
14. ______________________________
15. ______________________________
16. ______________________________
17. ______________________________
18. ______________________________

UNIT
14

Answer the questions beginning with the words given. The first two are done for you.

1. Which one do you want to sell?

   I don't know which one I want to sell.

2. Which boy had the best marks?

   I cannot tell you which boy had the best marks.

3. Which girl has the longest hair?

   I am not sure ______________________________________ .

4. Which one is the best?

   I am not sure ______________________________________ .

5. Which store sells toys?

   I will find out ______________________________________ .

6. Which book did he read last week?

   He has forgotten ______________________________________ .

7. Which book is she reading?

   She did not tell me ______________________________________ .

8. Which one would you like?

   I am not sure ______________________________________ .

9. Which dog barked at the mail carrier?

   No one knows ______________________________________ .

10. Which bus is going to Grandville?

    I will ask that man ______________________________________ .

11. Which boy finished first?

    No one told me ______________________________________ .

12. Which car is the fastest?

    I don't know ______________________________________ .

Combine the sentences.

1. I want to know something. Who broke the window?
   I want to know who broke the window.
2. I want to know something. Who wrote on the board?
   I want to know ______________________________ .
3. The teacher wants to know something. Who has read the book?
   The teacher ______________________________ .
4. The teacher does not know something. Who opened the window?
   The teacher ______________________________ .
5. I am trying to find out something. Who has my book?
   I ______________________________ .

Finish the sentences.

1. Who is that? Don't you know who that is?
2. Who is he? I don't know who he is.
3. Who is it? I don't know ______________________________ .
4. Who is she? I can't tell you ______________________________ .
5. Who was that? I did not see ______________________________ .
6. Who was it? I don't know ______________________________ .
7. Who were they? No one knows ______________________________ .
8. Who are they? I cannot tell you ______________________________ .
9. Who is he? We don't know ______________________________ .
10. Who was she? I will find out ______________________________ .
11. Who was he? My brother knows ______________________________ .
12. Who is she? Everyone knows ______________________________ .

UNIT 15

Read the sentences on page 35. For each one, find a sentence on this page with the same meaning. When you find one, write its number in the correct box on page 35. Then read the sentences again.

1. "What do you want?" we asked him.

2. "When will you finish painting the picture?" I asked her.

3. "What are you going to do next?" the teacher asked the boy.

4. "Which one do you like the most?" he asked her.

5. "I don't understand what you are saying," he said to her.

6. "How do you do it?" he asked her.

7. "Stop talking, please, and go on with your work!" the teacher said to her.

8. "How can I help you?" he asked her.

9. "I will tell you a secret if you promise not to tell anyone," she said to him.

10. "There are five words that I want you to learn," the teacher told them.

11. "I am feeling very happy," she told her friends.

12. "Put the table there, please," he said to the man.

13. "I don't know where my book is," she told the teacher.

14. "You will drop the cup if you are not careful," I said to her.

15. "I will not do it again," he promised his father.

16. "I don't think that I can answer the question," he said.

17. "Do you know the name of the flower?" he asked her.

18. "We will be home soon," his mother told him.

- [ ] The teacher asked the boy what he was going to do next.
- [ ] We asked him what he wanted.
- [ ] He told her that he did not understand what she was saying.
- [ ] I asked her when she would finish painting the picture.
- [ ] The teacher asked her to stop talking and to go on with her work.
- [ ] He asked her how he could help her.
- [ ] He asked her which one she liked the most.
- [ ] She told her friends that she was feeling very happy.
- [ ] He asked the man to put the table there.
- [ ] She said that she would tell him a secret if he promised not to tell anyone.
- [ ] He asked her how she did it.
- [ ] The teacher told them that there were five words that he wanted them to learn.
- [ ] I told her that she would drop the cup if she were not careful.
- [ ] She told the teacher that she did not know where her book was.
- [ ] He said that he did not think he could answer the question.
- [ ] He promised his father that he would not do it again.
- [ ] His mother told him that they would be home soon.
- [ ] He asked her if she knew the name of the flower.

UNIT 16

Write out the sentences giving the words spoken.

1. They asked the teacher when they could go.

   "When can we go?" they asked the teacher.

2. The man asked him what he wanted.

   "What do ____ .

3. He told his sister that he would not do it.

   "I ______________________________________," he said to his sister.

4. He asked his mother what he could buy.

   ____

5. He told the teacher that he did not know the answer.

   ____

6. The teacher told the class to put down their pens.

   ____

7. He told his mother that it was raining.

   ____

8. He asked her which one she wanted.

   ____

9. He asked his friend if he was going to leave school.

   ____

10. She asked him if he would like to have the book.

    ____

11. She asked him if he liked bananas.

    ____

12. He asked the woman if she needed help.

    ____

Write out the sentences and take out the quotation marks. Make any changes necessary.

1. "I don't know what to do," she said.

   She said that she did not know what to do.

2. "Do you play baseball?" she asked him.

   She asked him if ______________________________.

3. "Please put the book away," she said to him.

   She told him ______________________________.

4. "I don't think it is the right answer," she said.

   ____

5. "Will you buy me a new pen?" he asked his mother.

   ____

6. "How do you do it?" I asked him.

   ____

7. "What do you want?" she said to him.

   ____

8. "Where do you live?" she asked me.

   ____

9. "Why do you always come to school late?" the teacher asked him.

   ____

10. "Are you the oldest boy in the class?" she asked him.

    ____

11. "Which one do you like?" he asked her.

    ____

12. "It is very kind of you to help me," she said to him.

    ____

UNIT 17

For each pair of sentences, write one sentence with the same meaning.

1. He got home. Then he did his homework.

   After he got home, he did his homework.

2. She read one book. Then she got another from the library.

   After ______________________________ .

3. He finished reading the newspaper. Then he went to sleep.

   ______________ before ______________ .

4. He finished reading. Then he sat down.

   After ______________________________ .

5. He ate his dinner. Then he went out to play.

   ______________ before ______________ .

6. The teacher went outside. Then the children began to talk and play.

   After ______________________________ .

7. He did his work. Then he went to see his friend.

   ______________ before ______________ .

8. The teacher drew a picture on the board. Then the class copied it in their books.

   After ______________________________

   ______________________________ .

9. The examination began. Then she felt much better.

   After ______________________________ .

10. They swam for half an hour. Then they felt tired.

    ______________ before ______________ .

11. She went to sleep. Then her father came home.

    ______________ before ______________ .

12. She played baseball. Then she went swimming.

    ______________ before ______________ .

Write in the missing words. You can make these words by adding the parts of the words that you are given to the words underlined.

-less

1. They had no home. They were homeless.
2. He was completely without fear. He was ____________________ .
3. She did not do her work with care. She was ____________________ .
4. They did not have a child. They were ____________________ .

un-

5. The story they told was not true. It was ____________________ .
6. She said that she had not been happy for some time. She was ____________________ .
7. They wished that he were more kind to them. He was very ____________________ .

-ful

8. She always told the truth. She was a ____________________ girl.
9. There was plenty of color in the picture. It was very ____________________ .
10. He drove with great care. He was a very ____________________ driver.
11. The painting was full of beauty. It was very ____________________ . (Change *y* to *i*.)

-en

12. The boat was made of wood. It was a ____________________ boat.
13. The dress was made of wool. It was a ____________________ dress.
14. The little box was made of gold. It was a ____________________ box.

-al

15. She was very good at music. She was very ____________________ .
16. She dropped the plate by accident. It was quite ____________________ .

dis-

17. We must all be honest. No one likes a ____________________ person.
18. Most of the children were obedient but some were ____________________ .

You cannot go She must stay here They will not go home No one can go	until	you have finished. the lesson has ended. the teacher goes out. the bell rings.

Write fourteen sentences.

1. You cannot go until the bell rings.
2. They will not go home until ______________________________ .
3. ______________________________
4. ______________________________
5. ______________________________
6. ______________________________
7. ______________________________
8. ______________________________
9. ______________________________
10. ______________________________
11. ______________________________
12. ______________________________
13. ______________________________
14. ______________________________

Review

Rewrite each of the sentences in another way but do not change the meaning. You are given the beginning of each new sentence.

1. It was difficult to write in the dark.

   Writing in the dark was difficult.

2. Mike's desk is not as big as Alan's.

   Alan's desk ______________________________.

3. "You may go outside, boys and girls," said Miss Lane.

   Miss Lane let ______________________________.

4. "I want an ice cream cone," said Eva.

   Eva said that ______________________________.

5. We will not start until they are ready.

   We will start ______________________________.

6. "Where are you going, Terry?" said Bob.

   Bob asked Terry where ______________________________.

7. "What do you want?" he asked them.

   He asked ______________________________.

8. "Don't do it," the teacher said to them.

   The teacher ______________________________.

9. It was very heavy and we could not lift it.

   It was too ______________________________.

10. "Do you know what to do?" he said to her.

    He asked ______________________________.

11. The window was very small and he could not get through it.

    The window ______________________________.

12. "When are you going?" she asked him.

    She asked ______________________________.

UNIT 19

Write the sentences again using **should** *for* **ought to**, *and* **ought to** *for* **should**.

1. I think you ought to stop now.

   I think you should stop now.

2. I don't think you should tell her about it.

   I don't think you ought to tell her about it.

3. He ought to speak more slowly.

   ____

4. They ought not to make so much noise.

   ____

5. This school should have a bigger playground.

   ____

6. We ought not to put hot things where children can reach them.

   ____

7. We ought to brush our teeth twice a day.

   ____

8. Children should not play in the street.

   ____

9. Children ought not to play with sharp things.

   ____

10. We should help other people when we can.

    ____

11. Accidents should not happen.

    ____

12. We ought not to throw garbage on the ground.

    ____

Review

Draw a line under the best answer.

1. There is something wrong
A. to
B. with
C. for
D. of
E. by
this pen.

2. He was very angry
A. on
B. against
C. by
D. to
E. with
me.

3. He leaned the ladder
A. to
B. at
C. on
D. against
E. up
the wall and climbed up to the roof.

4. The teacher marked the books after she
A. collect
B. collection
C. corrected
D. collected
E. correct
them.

5. They thought that the film was very
A. excite.
B. excites.
C. excitement.
D. exciting.
E. excited.

6. When he left school, the principal gave him some good
A. advising.
B. advice.
C. advise.
D. advices.
E. advisings.

7. They did not think that the stories were
A. interestings
B. interest
C. interesting
D. interested
E. interests
because they had read them before.

UNIT 20

Combine the sentences.

1. He heard the news. He was very surprised.

   He was surprised to hear the news.

2. She saw him. She was very pleased.

   She was ____ .

3. They got to the top of the hill. They were very glad.

   ____

4. He did not jump. He was afraid.

   ____

5. He saw that she was unhappy. He was sorry.

   ____

6. He heard that she had hurt herself. He was very sorry.

   ____

7. She heard the good news. She was happy.

   ____

8. She heard that her brother had failed his examination. She was unhappy.

   ____

   ____

9. She heard that they could not come to the picnic. She was sorry.

   ____

10. He saw that it was raining. He was sorry.

    ____

11. He heard that tomorrow was a holiday. He was not sorry.

    ____

12. The students saw that it was the end of the exercise. They were pleased.

    ____

    ____

Write **get**, **got**, **gotten**, *or* **getting** *in the blank spaces.*

1. When I ________________ home from school, I have something to eat.
2. They ________________ into the car and drove away.
3. When we ________________ to school yesterday, we found that it was closed.
4. We always ________________ dressed before breakfast.
5. We tried to catch Joe's dog but it ________________ away.
6. She was sick last week but she soon ________________ better.
7. We will leave as soon as she has ________________ ready. She always takes a long time to ________________ ready.
8. When they ________________ to the town, they ________________ out of the bus.
9. "________________ out your books," the teacher said. "________________ ready to begin the lesson."
10. When they ________________ back from the picnic, it was ________________ dark.
11. "How are you doing?" he asked. "I have just ________________ married," she said.
12. "Go down to the store and ________________ me some rice," his mother said. "When you ________________ back, I'll cook you a nice meal."
13. It's nice to ________________ up in the morning but it's nicer to stay in bed!
14. By the time they had ________________ halfway up the hill, they were ________________ very tired.
15. The teacher ________________ up and walked out of the room after telling them to ________________ on with their work.
16. "________________ out of bed and ________________ your clothes on," his mother said.
17. We are ________________ near the end of the exercise. How many have you ________________ right?
18. Now we have ________________ to the end of the page.

UNIT 21

Complete the sentences using these words.

after	we reach the top of the hill.
	the bus comes.
when	someone opens the door.
	the clock says four o'clock.
	the other plane has landed.
until	she gets the letter.
	it rains.
before	you fall out of the boat.

1. She will be very pleased *when she gets the letter*.

2. He cannot go home ______________________________.

3. I will go inside ______________________________.

4. They will not leave the room ______________________________.

5. The plane will not take off ______________________________.

6. I think we will go home ______________________________.

7. Please sit down ______________________________.

8. We will have a rest ______________________________.

We will start They will tell me	after when	they all arrive. the signal is given. the food arrives. he gives the order. they find the map.
I will not begin Nothing can be done	before until	

Write eighteen sentences.

1. ______
2. ______
3. ______
4. ______
5. ______
6. ______
7. ______
8. ______
9. ______
10. ______
11. ______
12. ______
13. ______
14. ______
15. ______
16. ______
17. ______
18. ______

UNIT 22

Combine each sentence in two ways using **since**.

1. I had a good meal last when I went to the Golden Restaurant on Tuesday.
   I have not had a good meal since I went to the Golden Restaurant.
   I have not had a good meal since Tuesday.

2. I saw a snake last when we went to the zoo in June.
   ____
   ____

3. We went swimming last when my uncle took us out in his boat last year.
   ____
   ____

4. I went to the hospital last when I broke my arm in 1992.
   ____
   ____

5. We saw our teacher last when she said good-bye to us at the end of last term.
   ____
   ____

6. I ate an orange last when my mother gave me one on my birthday.
   ____
   ____

7. He read a book last when his father gave him one in December.
   ____
   ____

8. I saw a plane last when I went to the airport last month.
   ____
   ____

Underline the answer that makes a sentence with the same meaning.

1. I saw him last two weeks ago.

I have not seen him

A. it is two weeks.
B. for two weeks ago.
C. since two weeks.
D. for two weeks.
E. two weeks gone.

2. She has not been to the movies for three years.

She last went to the movies

A. for three years.
B. since three years.
C. three years ago.
D. for the past three years.
E. it is three years.

3. He came to school on Monday but he has not come since then.

He has not come to school [A. since / B. after / C. before / D. for / E. from] Monday.

A. since
B. after
C. before
D. for
E. from

4. I saw Jean last when she came to our apartment a week ago.

I have not seen Jean

A. since she came to our apartment.
B. since a week.
C. for a week ago.
D. after a week.
E. before she came to our apartment.

5. The children have not done any homework for four days.

The children did some homework last

A. four days ago.
B. since four days.
C. after four days.
D. in four days.
E. for four days.

UNIT 23

For each sentence write another sentence beginning with **It**.

1. Saying "Please" and "Thank you" is polite.
   It is polite to say "Please" and "Thank you."
2. Swimming by yourself is foolish.
   It is foolish ______________________________ .
3. Swimming after a heavy meal is unwise.
   ____
4. Working when a radio is playing is difficult.
   ____
5. Eating a heavy meal before going to bed is unwise.
   ____
6. Sleeping with all the windows closed is unhealthy.
   ____
7. Throwing garbage on the ground is against the law.
   ____
8. Standing up in a small boat is dangerous.
   ____
9. Running across a busy street is silly.
   ____
10. Going to bed late is bad for your health.
    ____
11. Playing with matches is dangerous.
    ____
12. Laughing at other people is very rude.
    ____

Rewrite each pair of sentences as one sentence. The first two have been done for you.

1. He could not come. We were very sorry.

We were very sorry that he could not come.

2. She has passed the test. I am pleased.

I am pleased that she has passed the test.

3. He has broken his leg. I am sorry.

I am sorry ____________________.

4. It did not rain today. I am glad.

I am glad ____________________.

5. Your answer is right. I am sure.

I am ____________________.

6. She is ill. I am sorry.

I am ____________________.

7. Tomorrow is a holiday. I am certain.

I ____________________.

8. She is feeling better. We are glad.

____

9. Our team will win. I am certain.

____

10. You cannot go on the picnic. I am sorry.

____

11. Your brother isn't well. I am sorry.

____

12. I have finished the page. I am glad.

____

UNIT 25

Rewrite each sentence using **less**. *Do not change the meaning.*

1. My book is more interesting than yours is.
   Your book is less interesting than mine is.
2. She was more polite than he was.
   He was less polite than she was.
3. He was more successful than she was.
   ____
4. My chair is more comfortable than yours is.
   ____
5. Your dog is more playful than mine is.
   ____
6. I am more forgetful than she is.
   ____
7. This corner is more dangerous than that corner is.
   ____
8. Our teacher is more cheerful than yours is.
   ____
9. Traveling by air is more exciting than traveling by sea.
   ____
10. Her book is more exciting than his is.
    ____
11. She is more obedient than her sister is.
    ____
12. Your classroom is more noisy than ours is.
    ____

Review

Underline the best answer.

1. A. That / B. It / C. He / D. Him / E. This — was kind of him to help us.

2. Is this book mine or is it one of A. your / B. you / C. your's / D. yours / E. yours' , Joe?

3. The toy boat was made A. by / B. into / C. off / D. of / E. out tin.

4. He stood outside the door A. since / B. for / C. while / D. in / E. during ten minutes.

5. She A. shake / B. shaked / C. shaken / D. shooked / E. shook the box to hear if there was anything inside.

6. Sarah did not know where A. to put it. / B. will I put it. / C. she will put it. / D. will she put it. / E. will I put it?

7. The band will begin to play when the President A. arrive. / B. arrives. / C. was arriving. / D. arrived. / E. will arrive.

UNIT 26

Answer the questions.

1. 

What has he done?

He has hurt himself.

2. 

Who is she looking at?

She ______________________________.

3. 

Who is he laughing at?

He ______________________________.

4. 

Who are they laughing at?

They ______________________________.

5. 

Who is she washing?

____

6. 

Who is it washing?

____

7. 

Who is the dog shaking?

____

8. 

What have they done?

____

Complete the sentences.

1. A cat never needs a bath. It is always washing ____________________ .
2. There is no need to stop this machine. When it has finished, it stops ____________________ .
3. She stood on her toes so that she could see ____________________ in the mirror.
4. "Your face is dirty," said Mike's mother. "I wish you could see ____________________ ."
5. If you play with a sharp knife, you may cut ____________________ .
6. People who live alone sometimes talk to ____________________ .
7. He lifted ____________________ up with his hands and climbed over the wall.
8. The boys fell down the hill and hurt ____________________ .
9. The mother of the two boys told them to look after ____________________ while they were away.
10. "There is plenty of food," she told the children. "Help ____________________ !"

Finish the questions. The first three have been done for you.

1. It is a very big school, *isn't it*?
2. You bought something at that store, *didn't you*?
3. He didn't give us any homework to do, *did he*?
4. It rained a lot last night, ____________________ ?
5. She doesn't go to that school anymore, ____________________ ?
6. It's a long way from Japan to New York, ____________________ ?
7. It isn't a very big school, ____________________ ?
8. You are going to leave school next term, ____________________ ?

Review

Complete sentence (b). It must have the same meaning as sentence (a).

1. (a) She sings as sweetly as a bird.
(b) She sings like ______________________________ .

2. (a) He swims as well as a fish.
(b) He swims ______________________________ .

3. (a) Our apartment is different from your apartment.
(b) Our apartment is not ______________________________ .

4. (a) I came here at eight o'clock.
(b) I have been here ______________________________ .

5. (a) It is now ten o'clock. She went out at eight o'clock.
(b) She went out two ______________________________ .

6. (a) There is a lot of homework that I must do tonight.
(b) I have ______________________________ .

7. (a) I must help my mother before I go to school.
(b) I have ______________________________ .

8. (a) We need more pencils.
(b) There are ______________________________ .

9. (a) The plate is not big enough for all the fruit on it.
(b) There is too ______________________________ .

10. (a) There are forty boys in the classroom but only thirty desks.
(b) There are too ______________________________ .

11. (a) We cannot carry the box through the door because the box is too big.
(b) The box is ______________________________ .

12. (a) The radio will go into a pocket because it is very small.
(b) The radio is small ______________________________ .

Review

Complete sentence (b). It must have the same meaning as sentence (a).

1. (a) "What should I do?" Jim said to Kathy.

(b) Jim asked Kathy what ______________________________.

2. (a) "Where should I put the books?" Jean asked Mrs. Wilson.

(b) Jean asked Mrs. Wilson where ______________________________.

3. (a) "I have a cold," said Eva.

(b) Eva said that ______________________________.

4. (a) "I like ice cream," Alan said.

(b) Alan said that ______________________________.

5. (a) "We know the answer," the students said.

(b) The students said that ______________________________.

6. (a) "What are the men doing?" Mr. Mitchell wanted to know.

(b) Mr. Mitchell wanted to know what ______________________________.

7. (a) "How old are you, David?" asked Marie.

(b) Marie asked David how ______________________________.

8. (a) We asked her where it was and she told us.

(b) She told us ______________________________.

9. (a) "Why do you want a bicycle?" Bob's mother asked him.

(b) Bob's mother asked him why ______________________________.

10. (a) She wants a dress but I don't know which one.

(b) I don't know ______________________________.

11. (a) "Who is that man?" she asked her sister.

(b) She asked her sister who ______________________________.

12. (a) "Are you feeling well, Marie?" the teacher asked.

(b) The teacher asked Marie if ______________________________.

Review

Complete sentence (b). It must have the same meaning as sentence (a).

1. (a) "Do you want any more?" she asked the children.
(b) She asked the children if ______________________________.

2. (a) He finished the book before he went to bed.
(b) After he ______________________________.

3. (a) After she closed all the windows, she went out.
(b) She closed ______________________________.

4. (a) When the lights turned green, they crossed the road.
(b) They did not cross the road ______________________________.

5. (a) You ought to write more carefully.
(b) You should ______________________________.

6. (a) I cannot jump into the water because I am afraid.
(b) I am afraid ______________________________.

7. (a) We can begin when Jack gets here.
(b) We cannot begin ______________________________.

8. (a) I saw him last when he left school.
(b) I have not ______________________________.

9. (a) Swimming underwater is not easy.
(b) It is ______________________________.

10. (a) We have almost finished the page and I am glad.
(b) I am glad ______________________________.

11. (a) A hurricane is more dangerous than a thunderstorm.
(b) A thunderstorm is ______________________________.

12. (a) Your glass is less full than mine is.
(b) My glass is ______________________________.